Films
Remastered
Posters

vol. 1

Iacob Adrian

ISBN-13 : 978-1480298620
ISBN-10 : 148029862X

Dtp
and
graphic design

Iacob Adrian

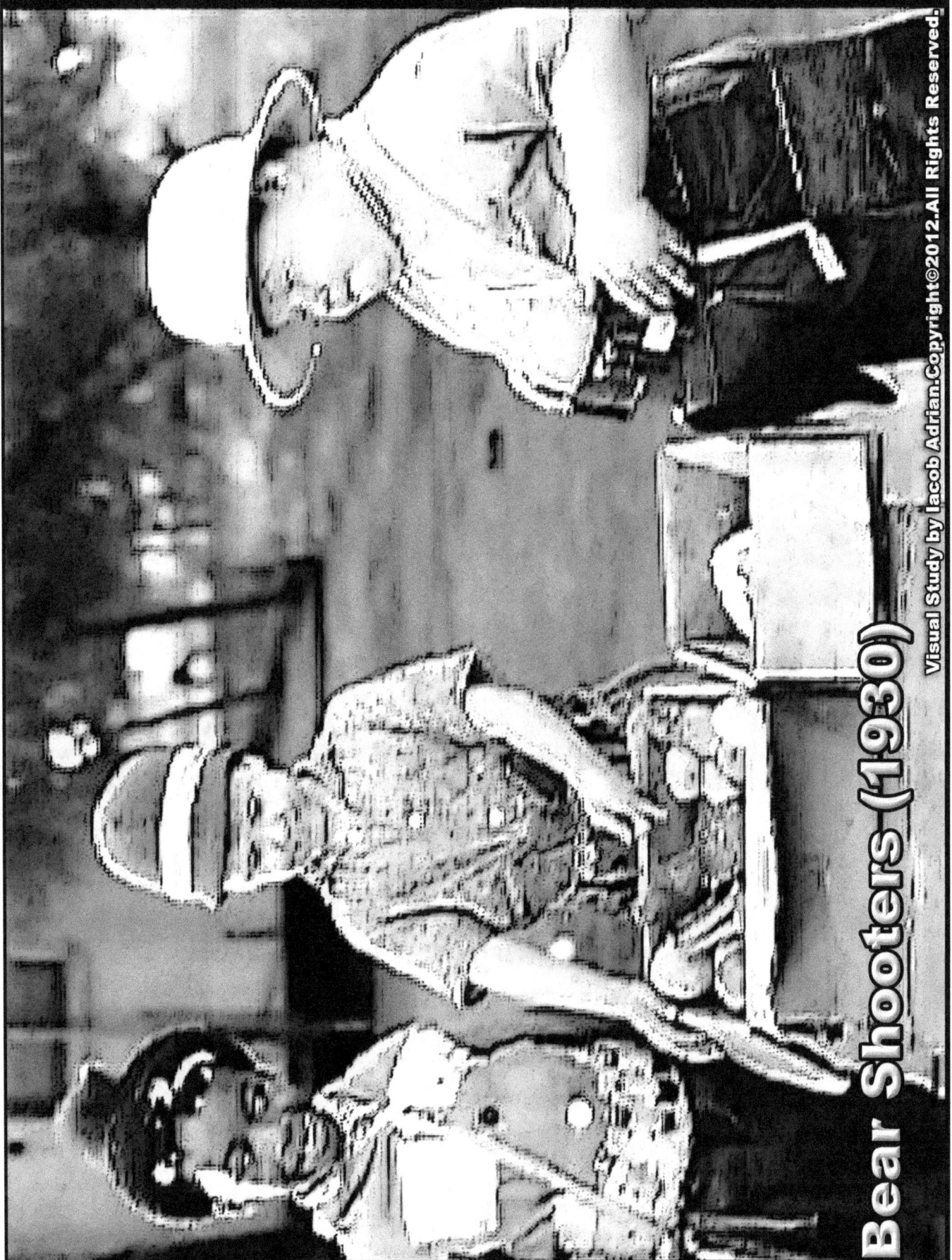

Bear Shooters (1930)

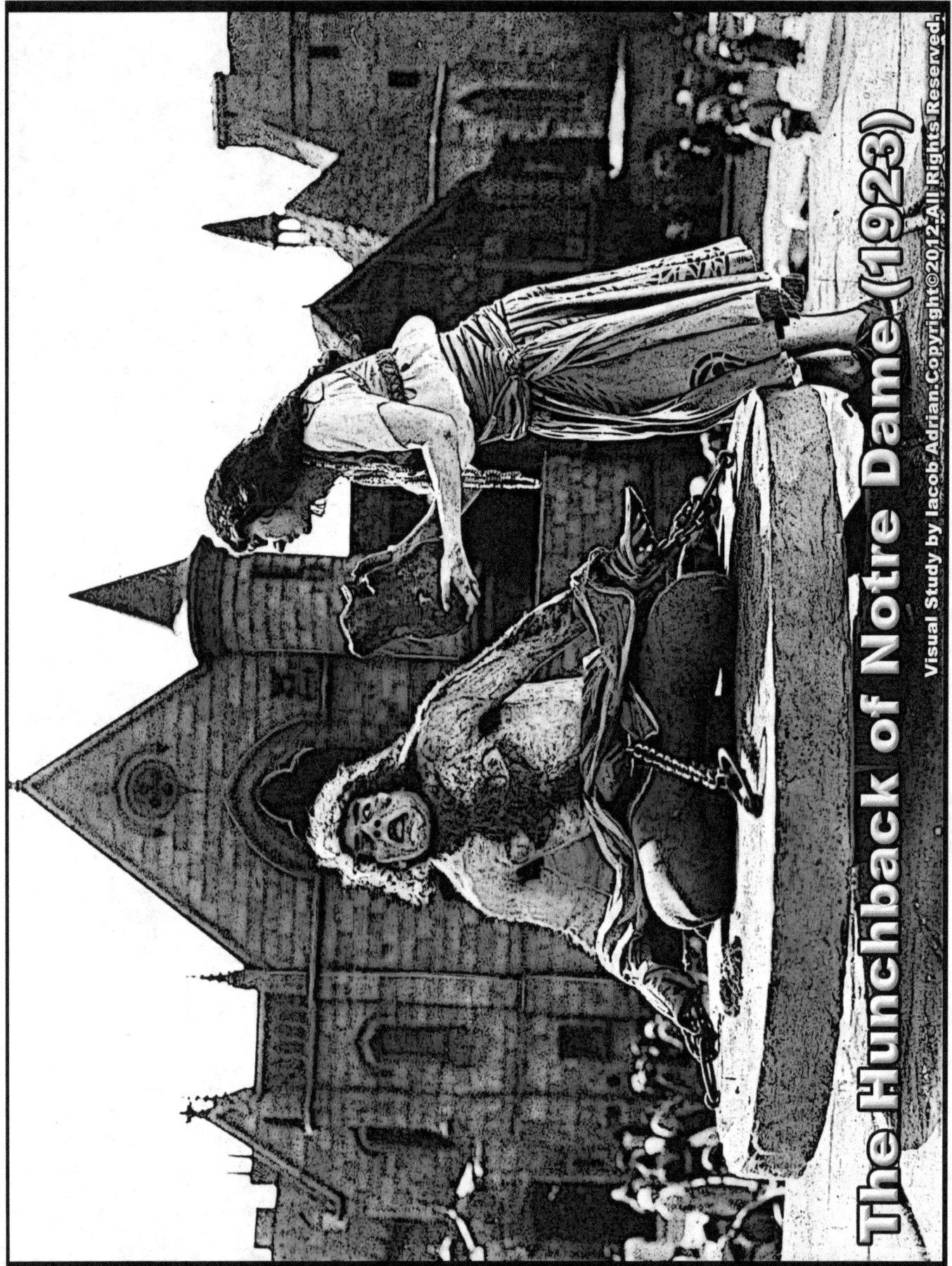

The Hunchback of Notre Dame (1923)

John Barrymore

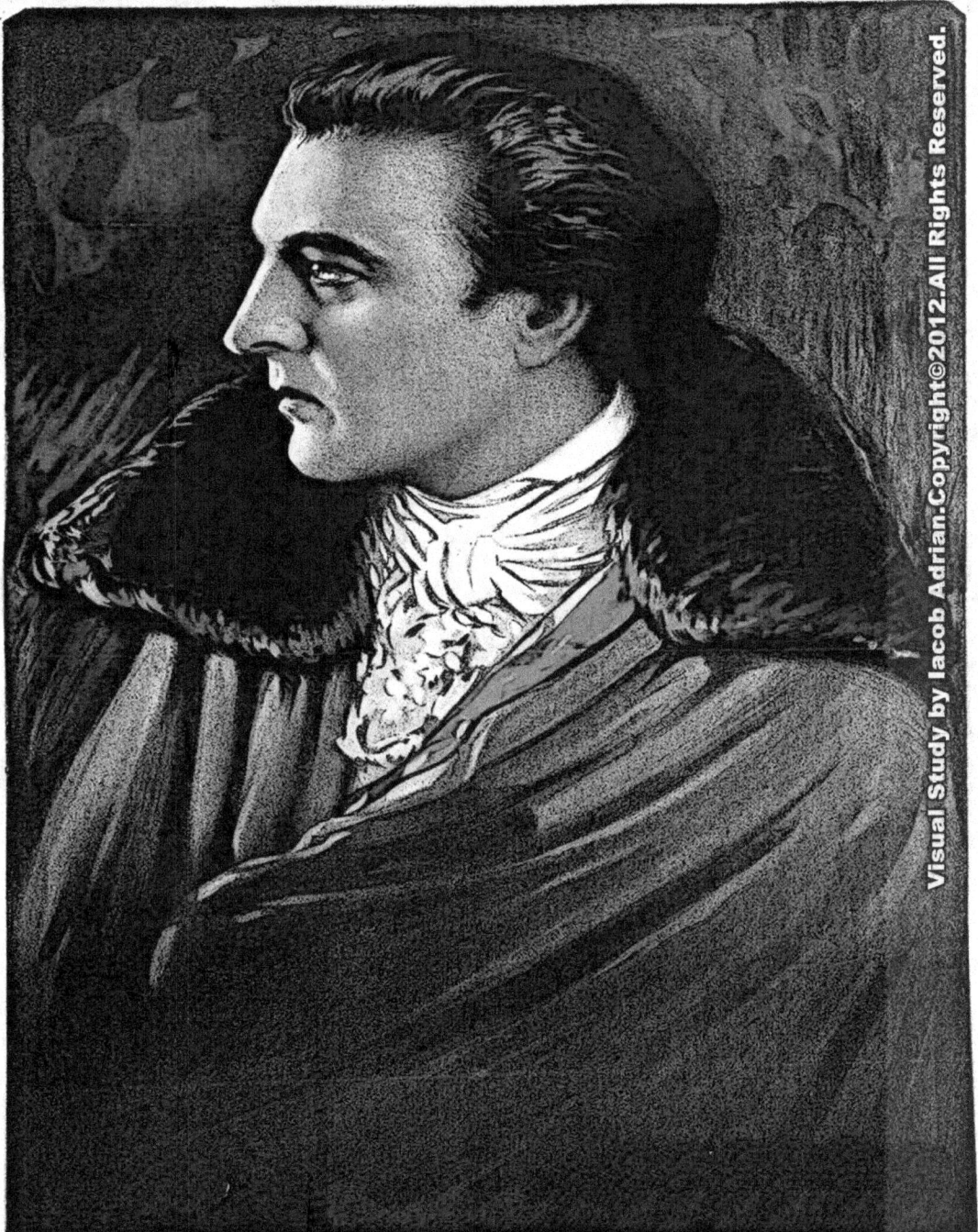

IN

"BEAU BRUMMEL"

BY ARRANGEMENT WITH MRS. RICHARD MANSFIELD

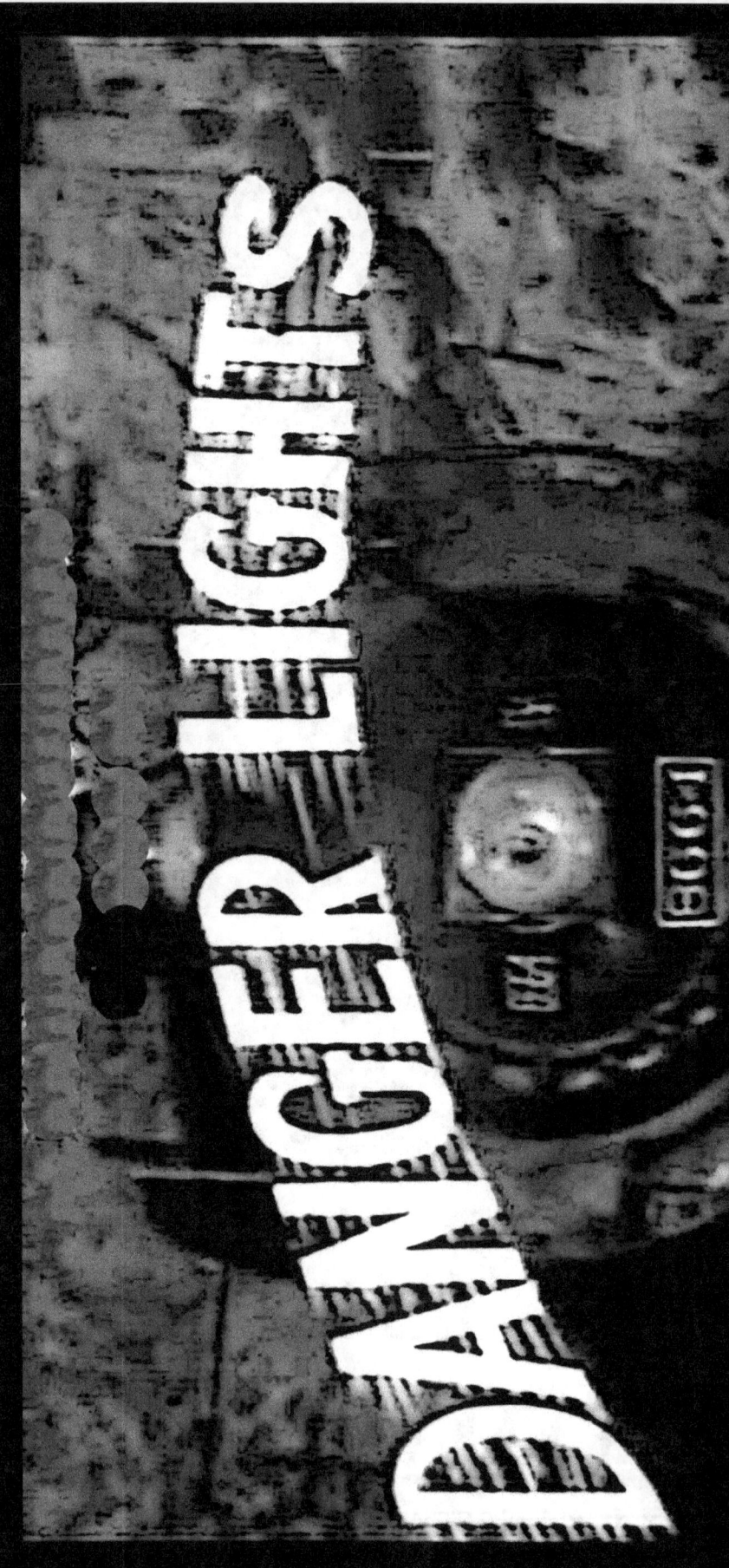

Danger Lights (1930)

the 3 STOOGES

MOE · CURLY · LARRY

Disorder in the Court

Produced by Jules White
Directed by Preston Black
Story and Screen Play by Felix Adler

Ciociara

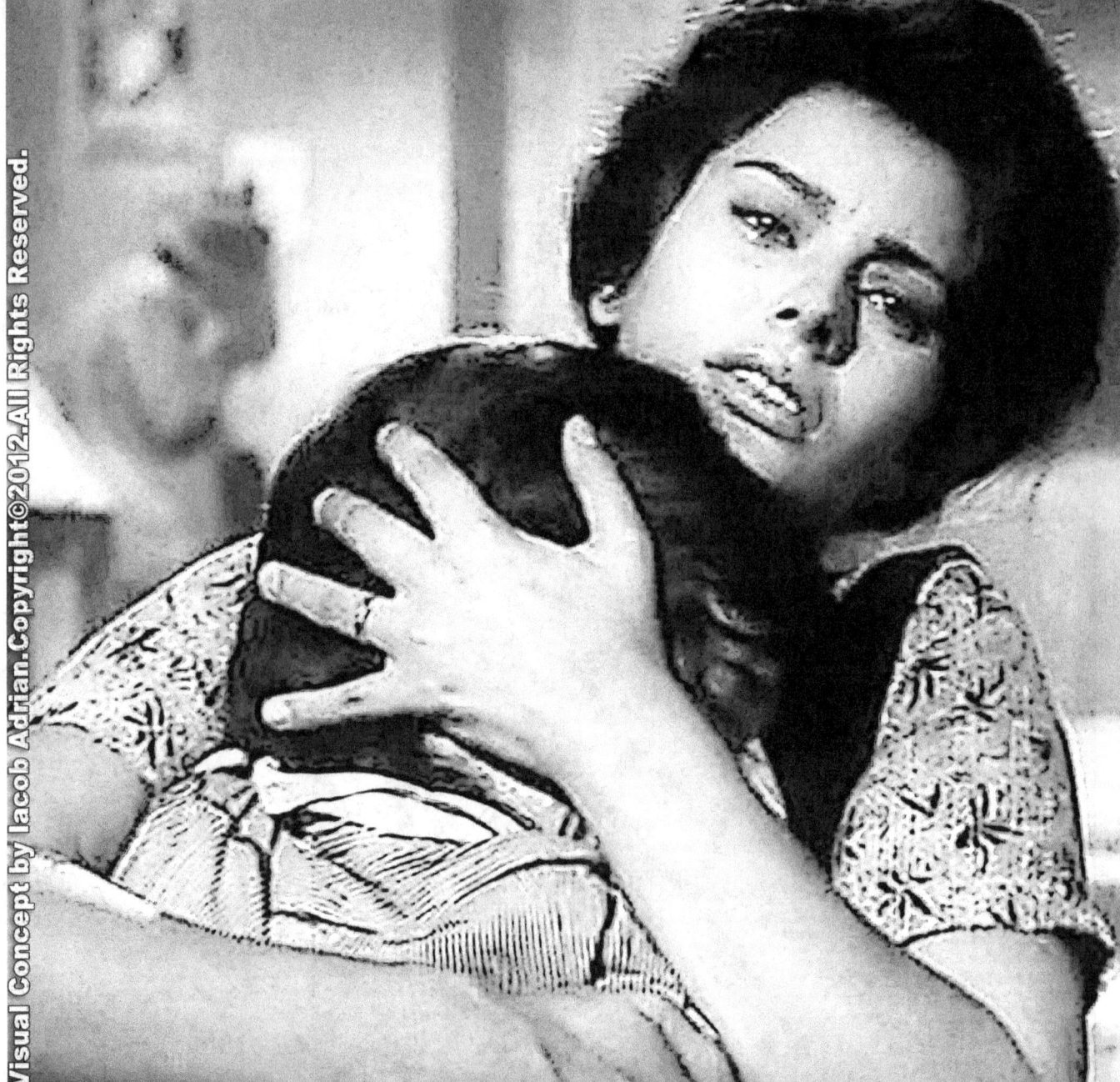

Sophia Loren

Jean-Paul Belmondo   Eleonora Brown

PRODUCER Iacob Adrian   "La Ciociara (Two Women)" (1960)
ISAN : 0000-0003-5B47-0000-O-0000-0000-2   Remastered audio & video version
First release

LESLIE HOWARD

IN

W. SOMERSET MAUGHAM'S
WORLD FAMOUS NOVEL

"OF HUMAN BONDAGE"

with

BETTE DAVIS

FRANCES DEE
KAY JOHNSON
REGINALD DENNY

DIRECTED BY JOHN CROMWELL
A PANDRO S. BERMAN
PRODUCTION

"COUNTRY OF ORIGIN U.S.A."

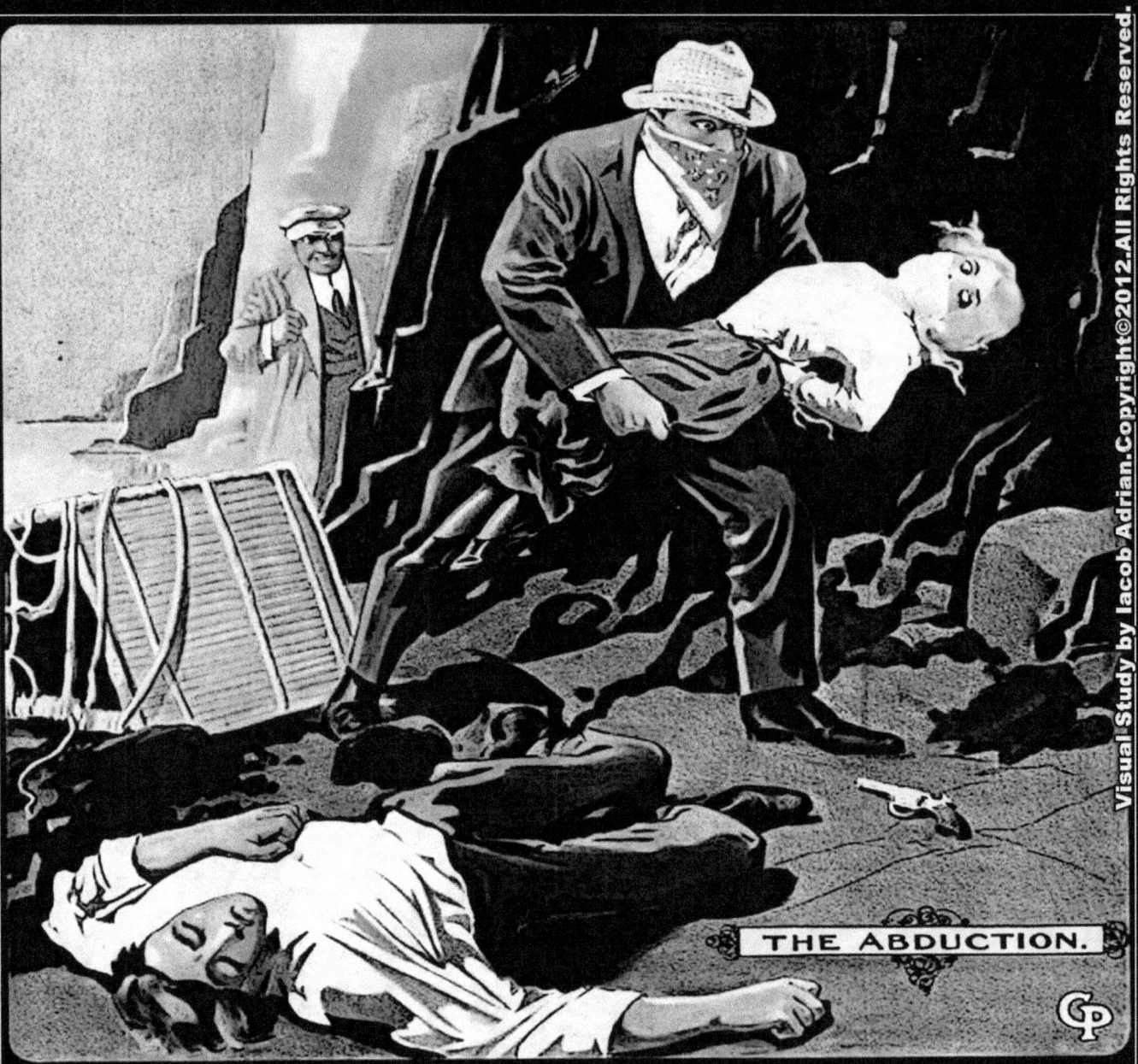

THE ABDUCTION.

THE ECLECTIC FILM COMPANY'S
GREAT $ 25.000 PRIZE PHOTO PLAY
THE PERILS
OF
PAULINE
6 TH EPISODE IN 2 PARTS

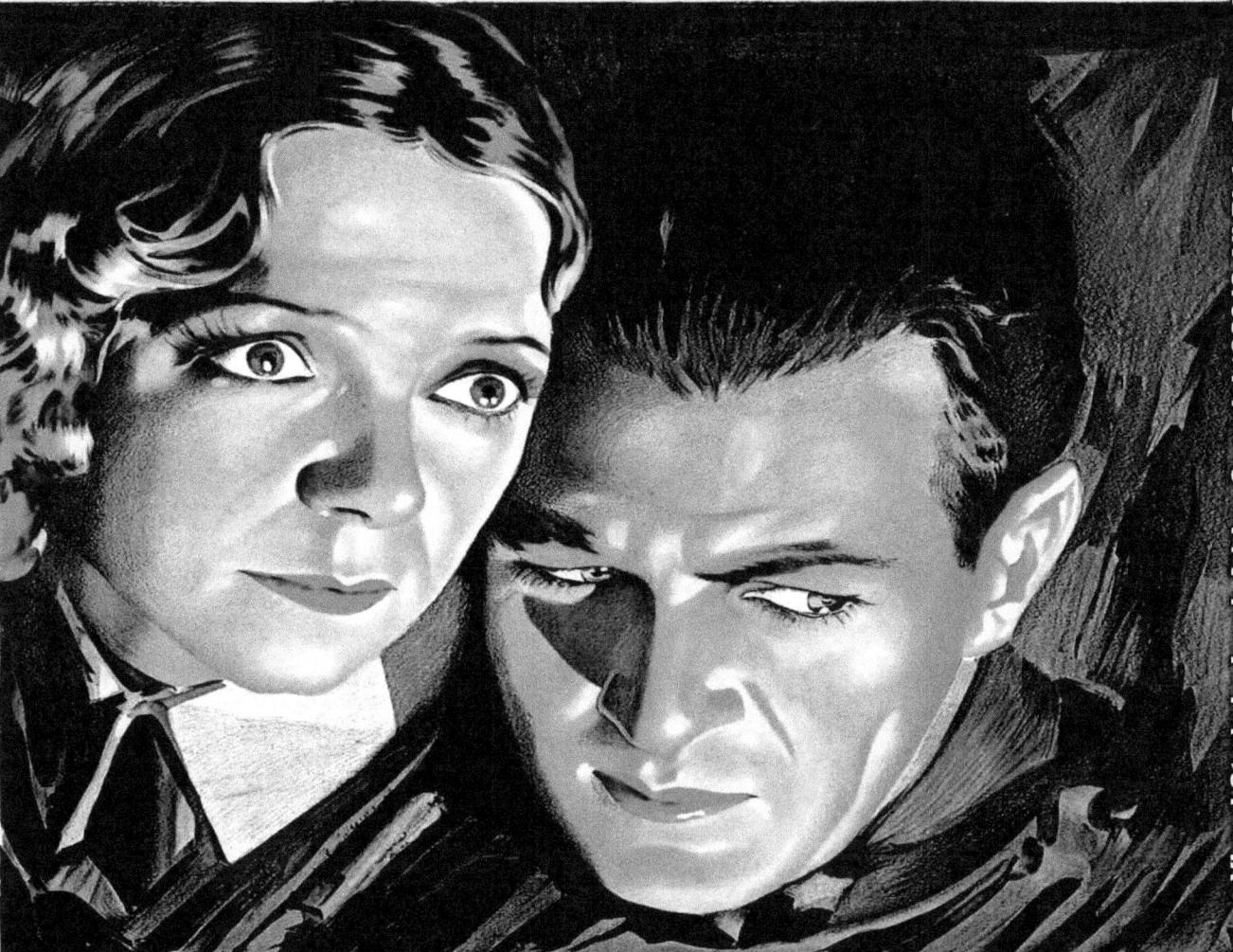

A FAREWELL TO ARMS

With

HELEN HAYES
GARY COOPER AND ADOLPHE MENJOU

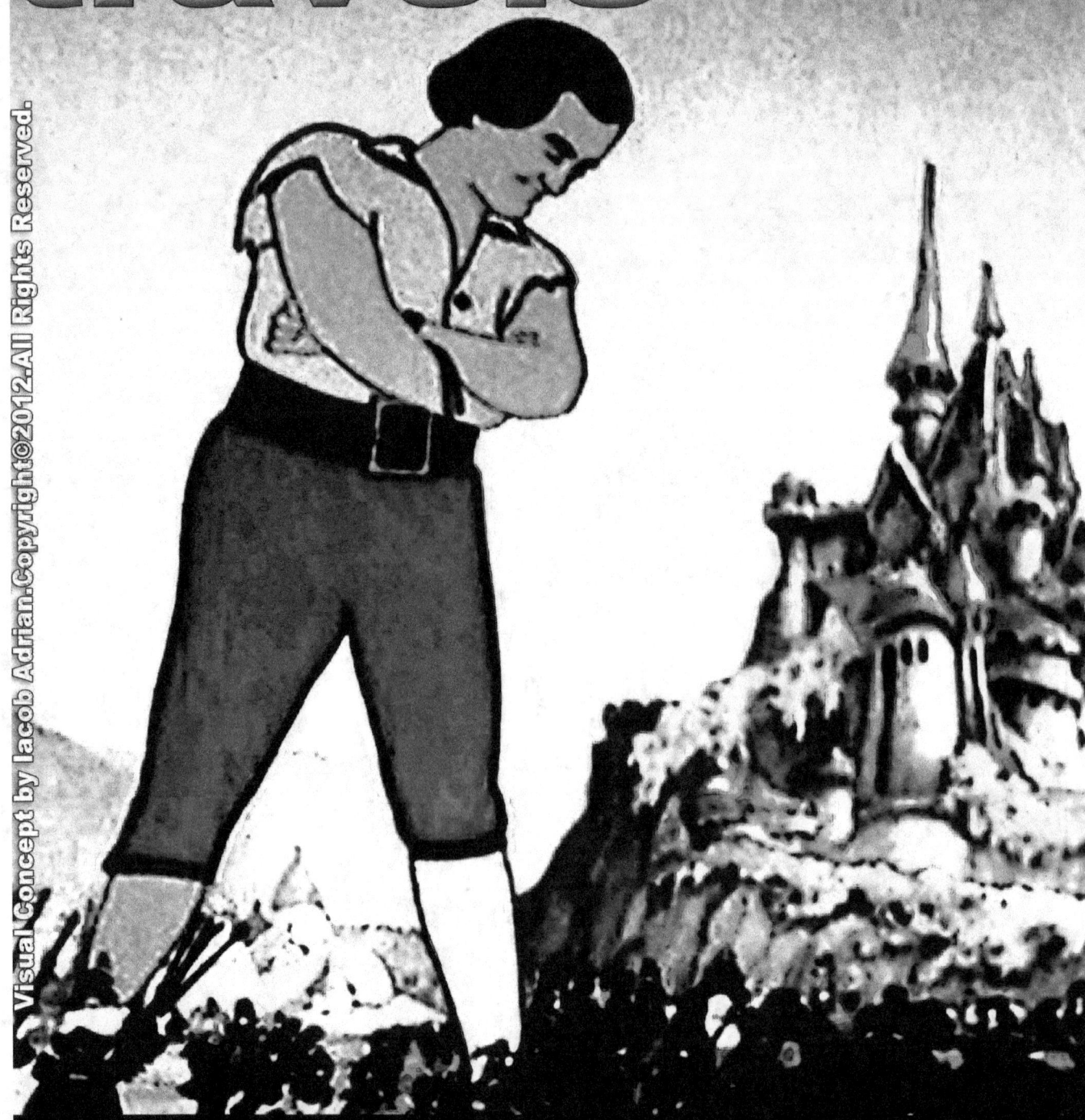

Gulliver travels

PRODUCER Iacob Adrian
ISAN : 0000-0003-58F9-0000-5-0000-0000-M

"Gulliver's Travels" (1939)
Remastered audio & video version
First release

RKO Radio Pictures

DAVID O. SELZNICK

A LOVE TOO SACRED TO BE HELD IN MARRIAGE BONDS

ANN HARDING
LESLIE HOWARD
in
THE ANIMAL KINGDOM

with
MYRNA LOY · WILLIAM GARGAN
NEIL HAMILTON
HENRY STEPHENSON · ILKA CHASE

FROM THE PLAY BY
PHILIP BARRY

DIRECTED BY
EDWARD H. GRIFFITH

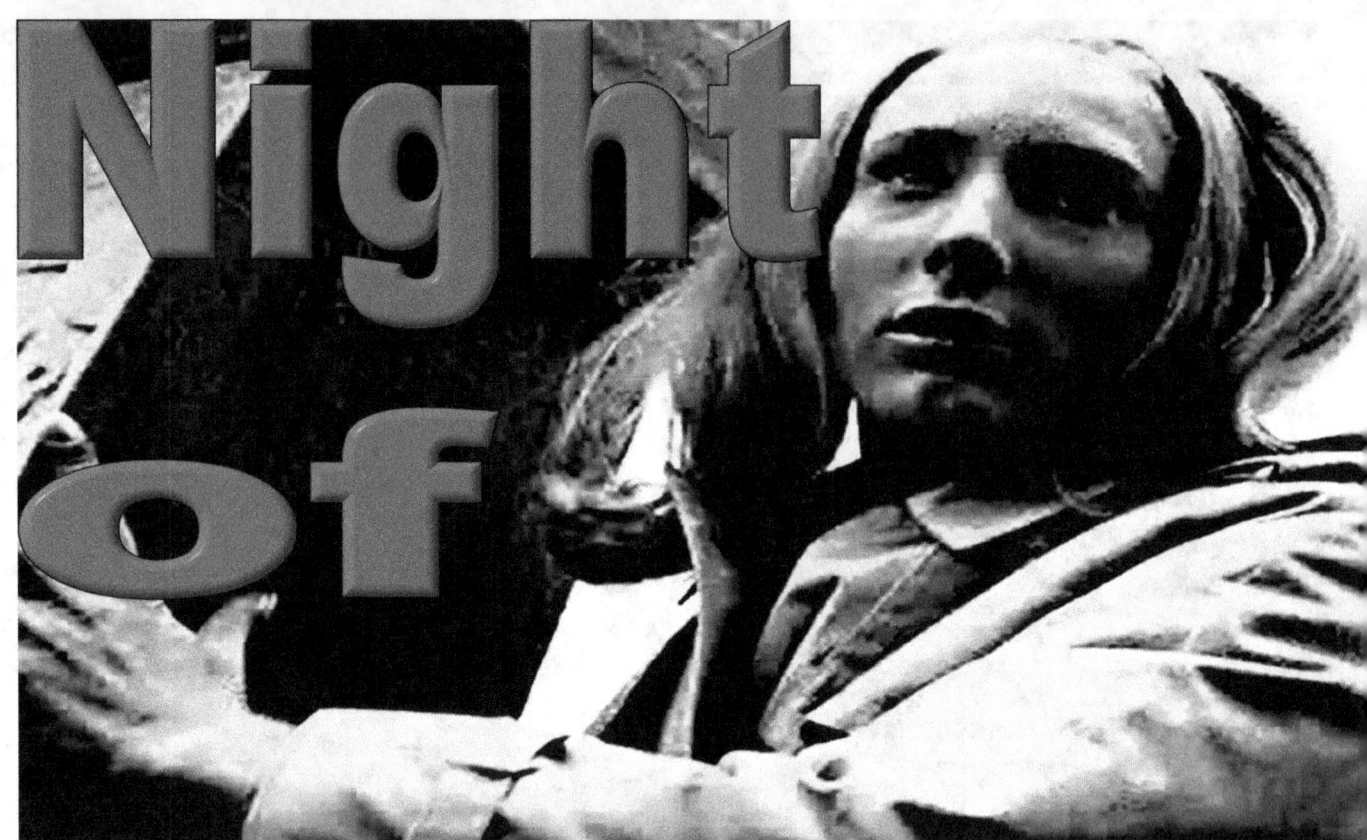

Night of the Dead

"Night of the Living Dead" (1968)
Remastered audio & video version
First release

FRANK
CAPRA'S
Production

GARY
COOPER ★ BARBARA STANWYCK

Meet John Doe

EDWARD
ARNOLD · WALTER BRENNAN
SPRING BYINGTON · JAMES GLEASON · GENE LOCKHART
Screen Play by
ROBERT RISKIN
Directed by
FRANK CAPRA

WITH THESE ZOMBIE EYES
he rendered her powerless

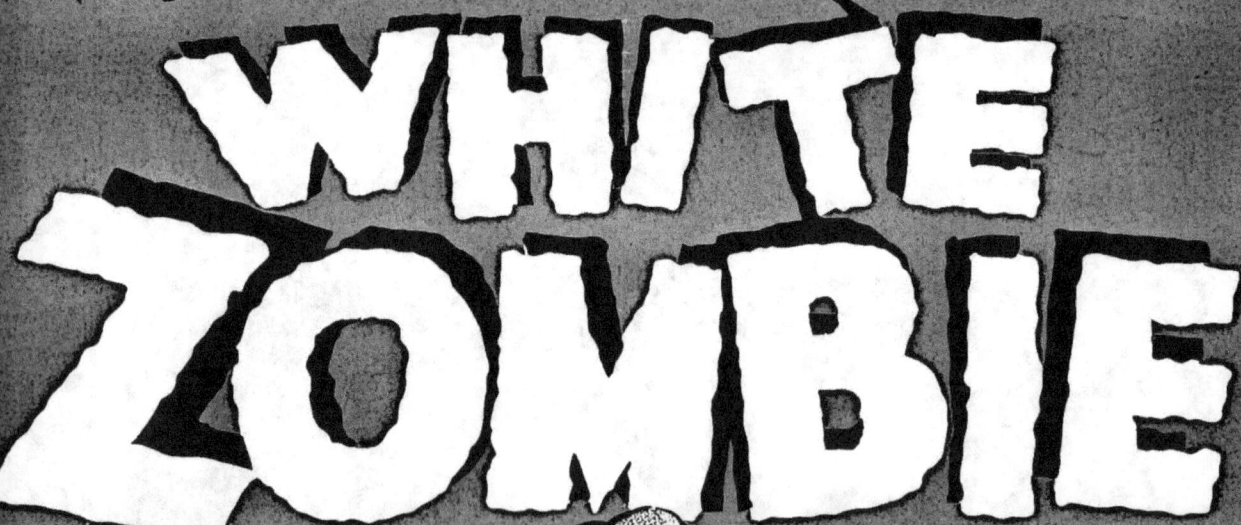

WHITE ZOMBIE

WITH THIS ZOMBIE GRIP
he made her perform his every desire!

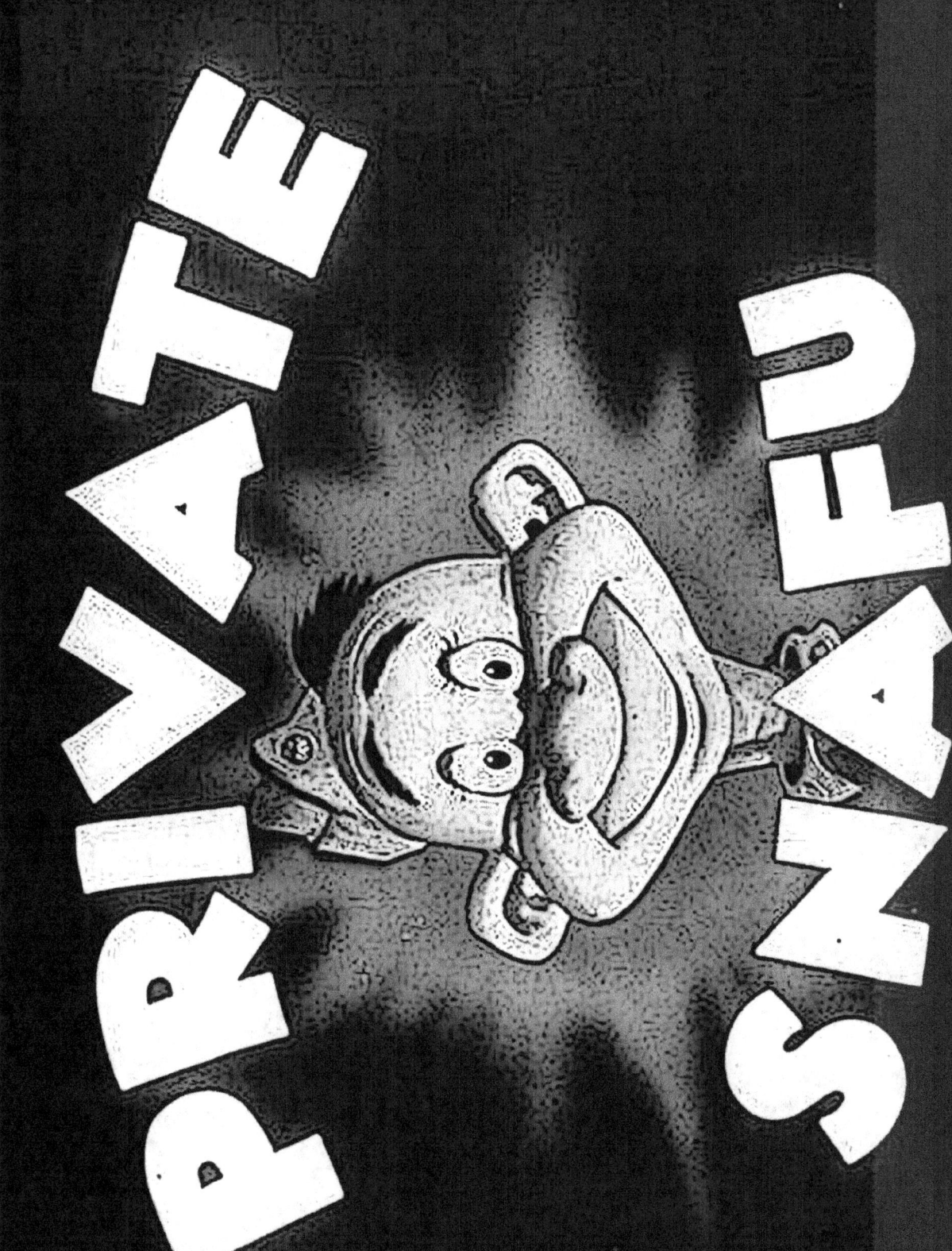

PRIVATE SNAFU

-1943-1946

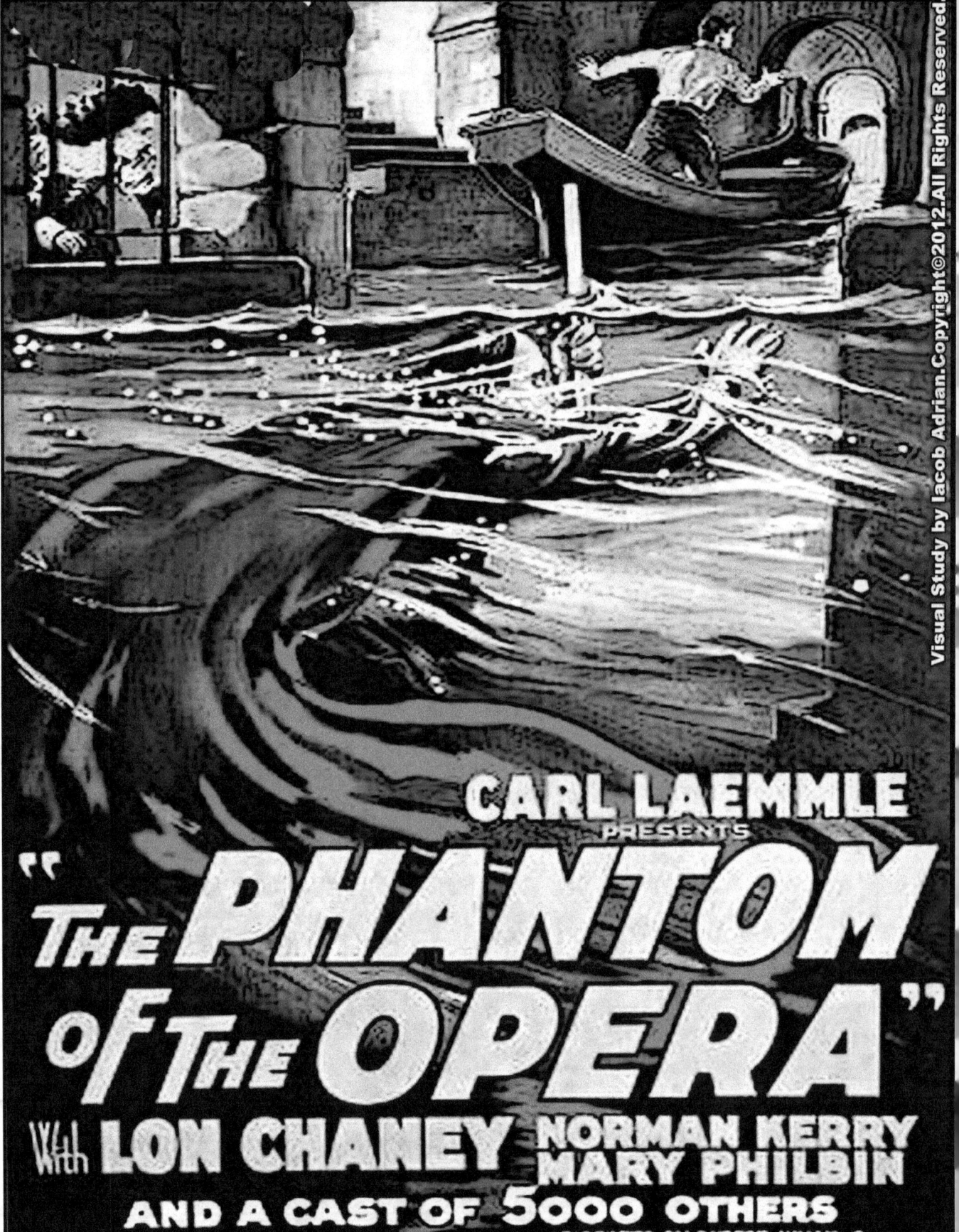

CARL LAEMMLE
PRESENTS
"THE PHANTOM OF THE OPERA"
WITH LON CHANEY NORMAN KERRY MARY PHILBIN
AND A CAST OF 5000 OTHERS
STORY BY GASTON LEROUX   DIRECTED BY RUPERT JULIAN

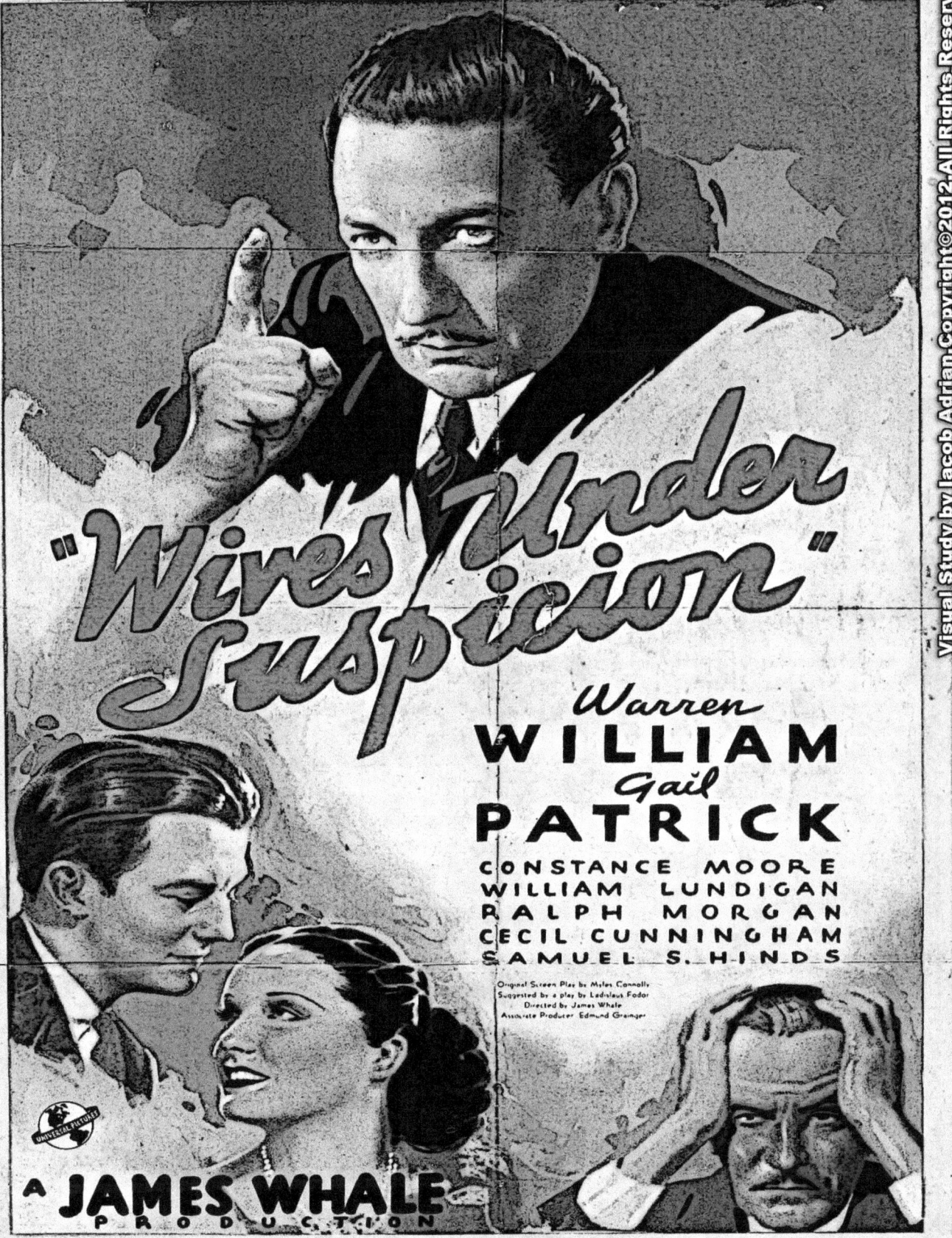

"Wives Under Suspicion"

Warren **WILLIAM**

Gail **PATRICK**

CONSTANCE MOORE
WILLIAM LUNDIGAN
RALPH MORGAN
CECIL CUNNINGHAM
SAMUEL S. HINDS

Original Screen Play by Myles Connolly
Suggested by a play by Ladislaus Fodor
Directed by James Whale
Associate Producer Edmund Grainger

A **JAMES WHALE** PRODUCTION

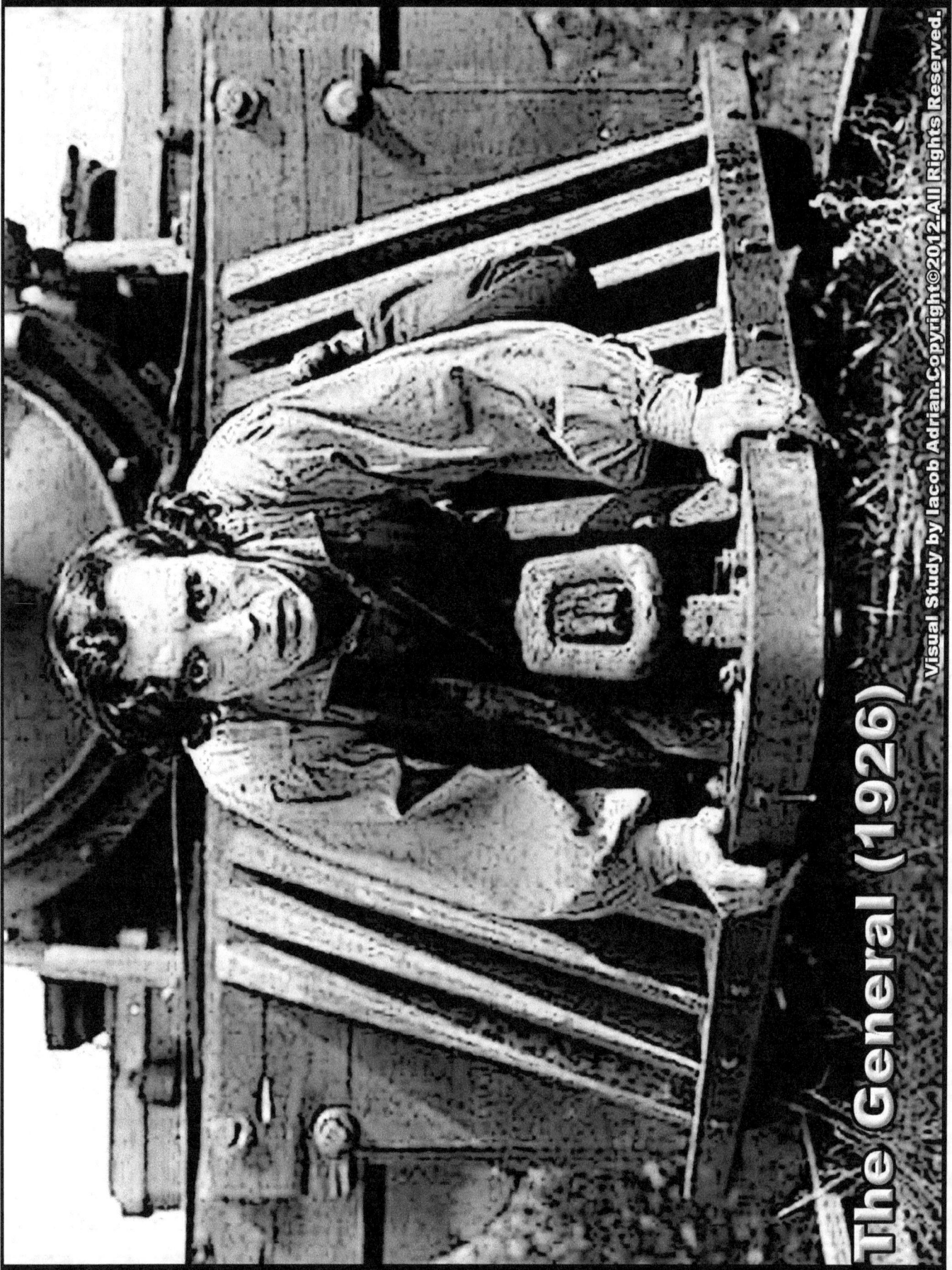

The General (1926)

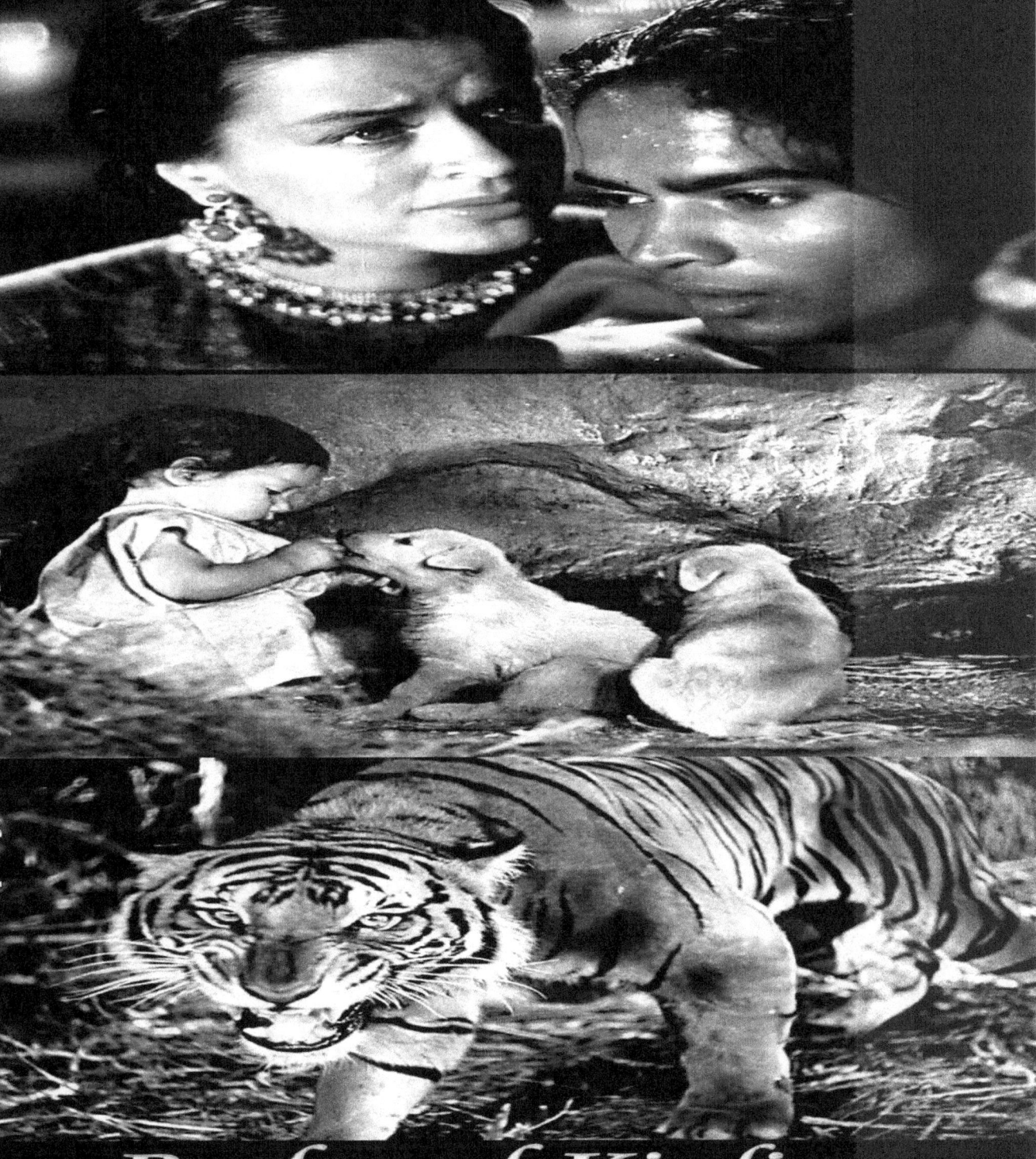

The Jungle Book

Rudyard Kipling

PRODUCER Iacob Adrian
ISAN : 0000-0003-5AF0-0000-5-0000-0000-M

"Jungle Book" (1942)
Remastered audio & video version
First release

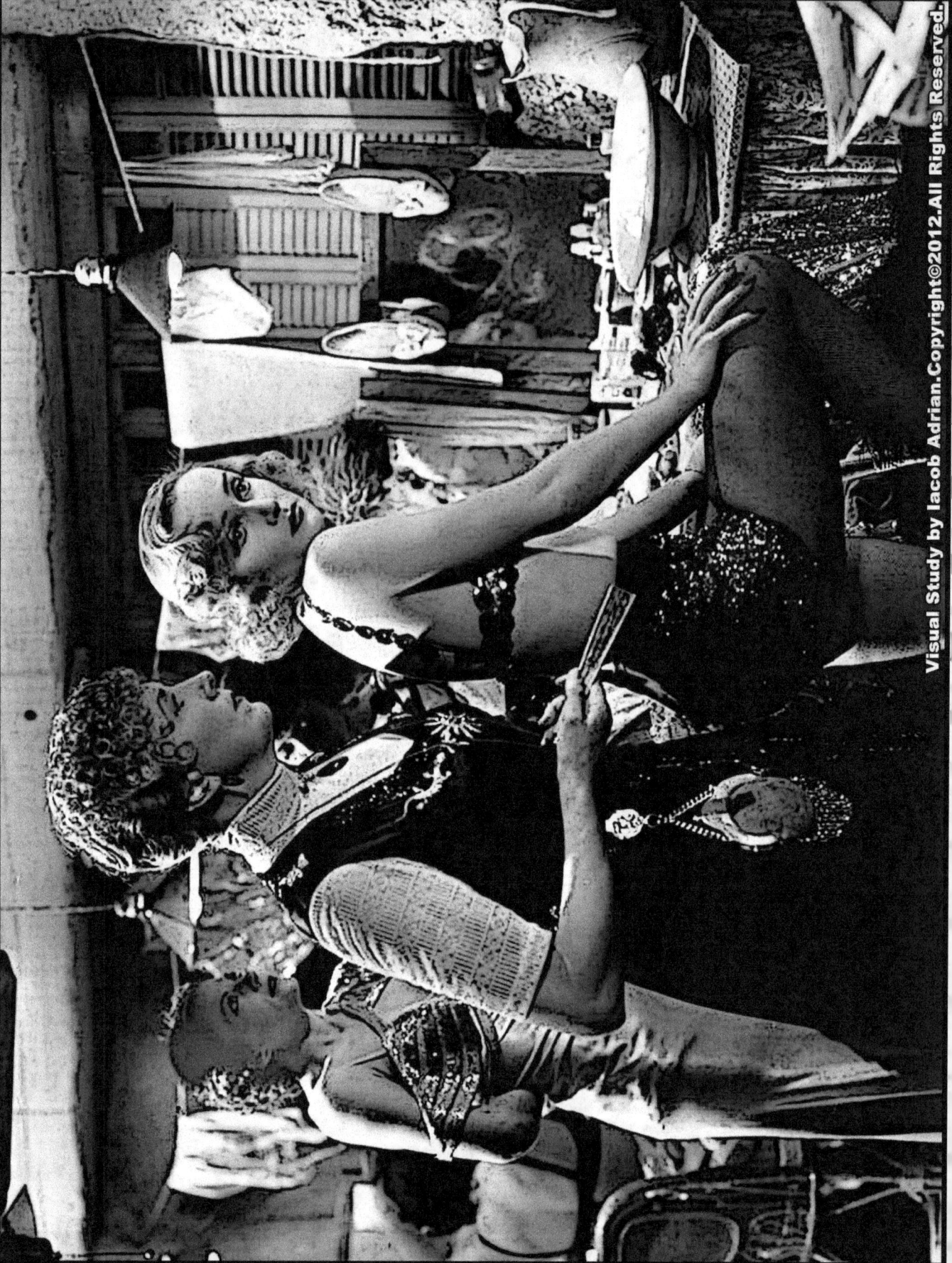

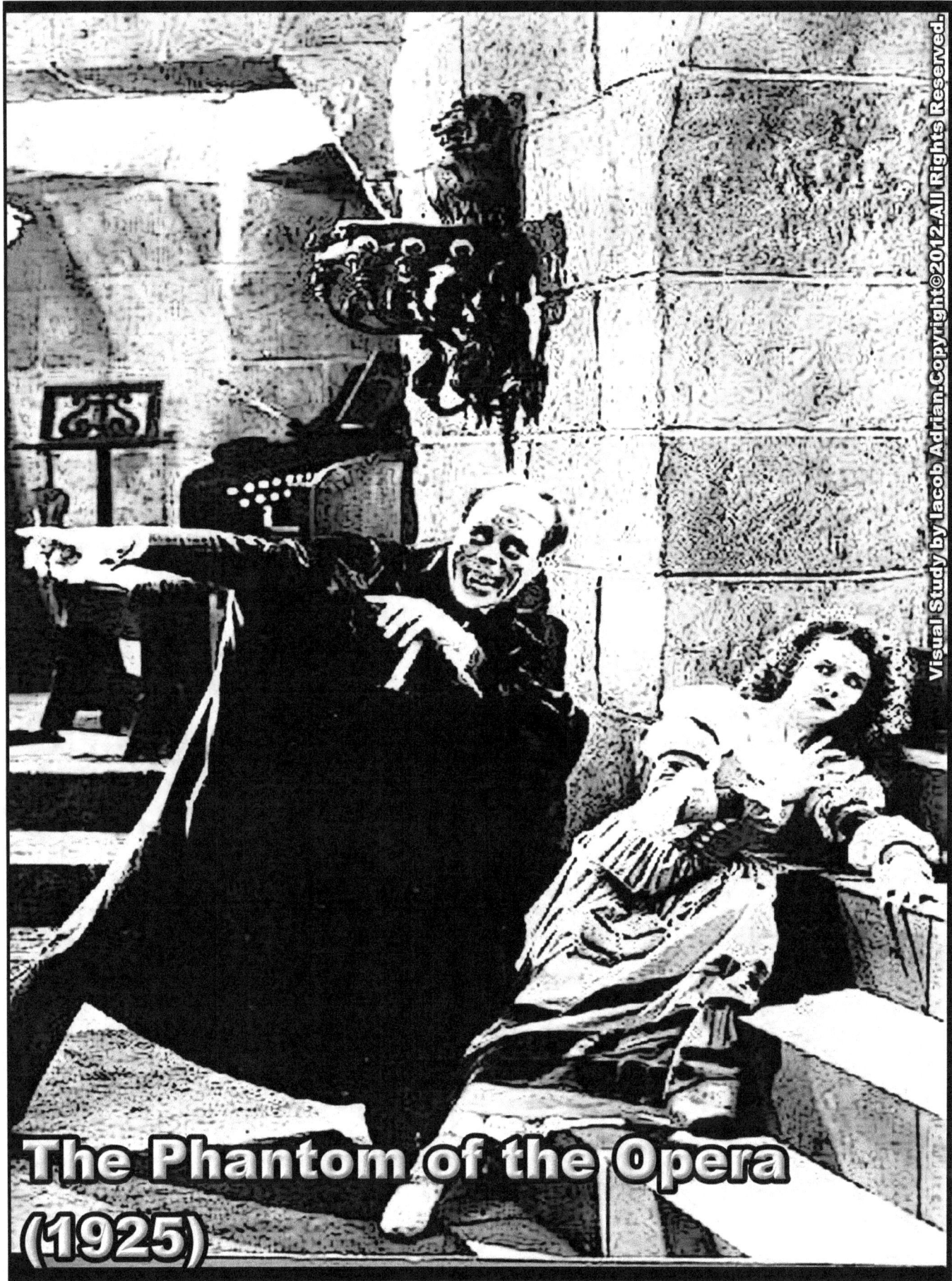

The Phantom of the Opera (1925)

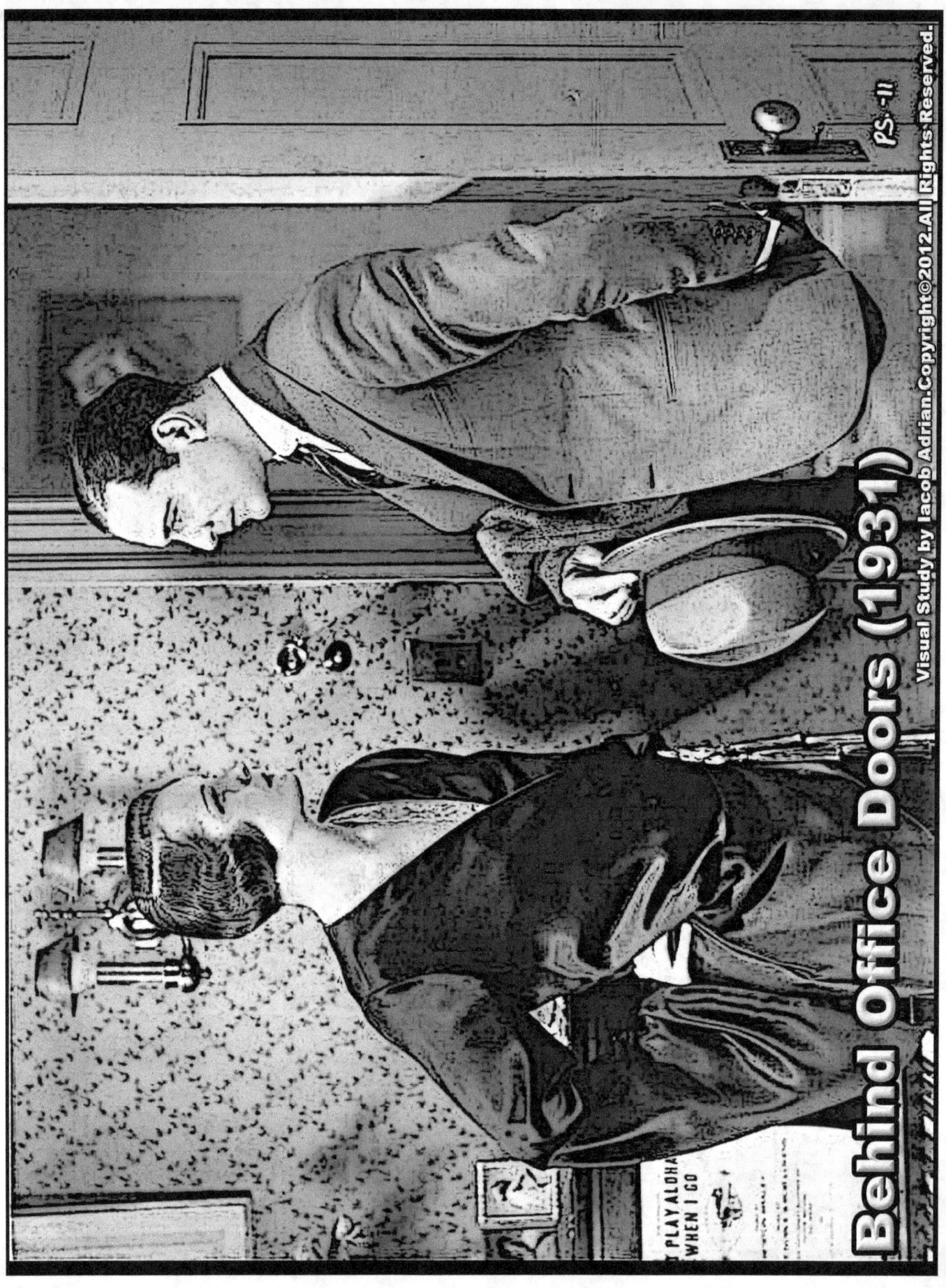

Behind Office Doors (1931)

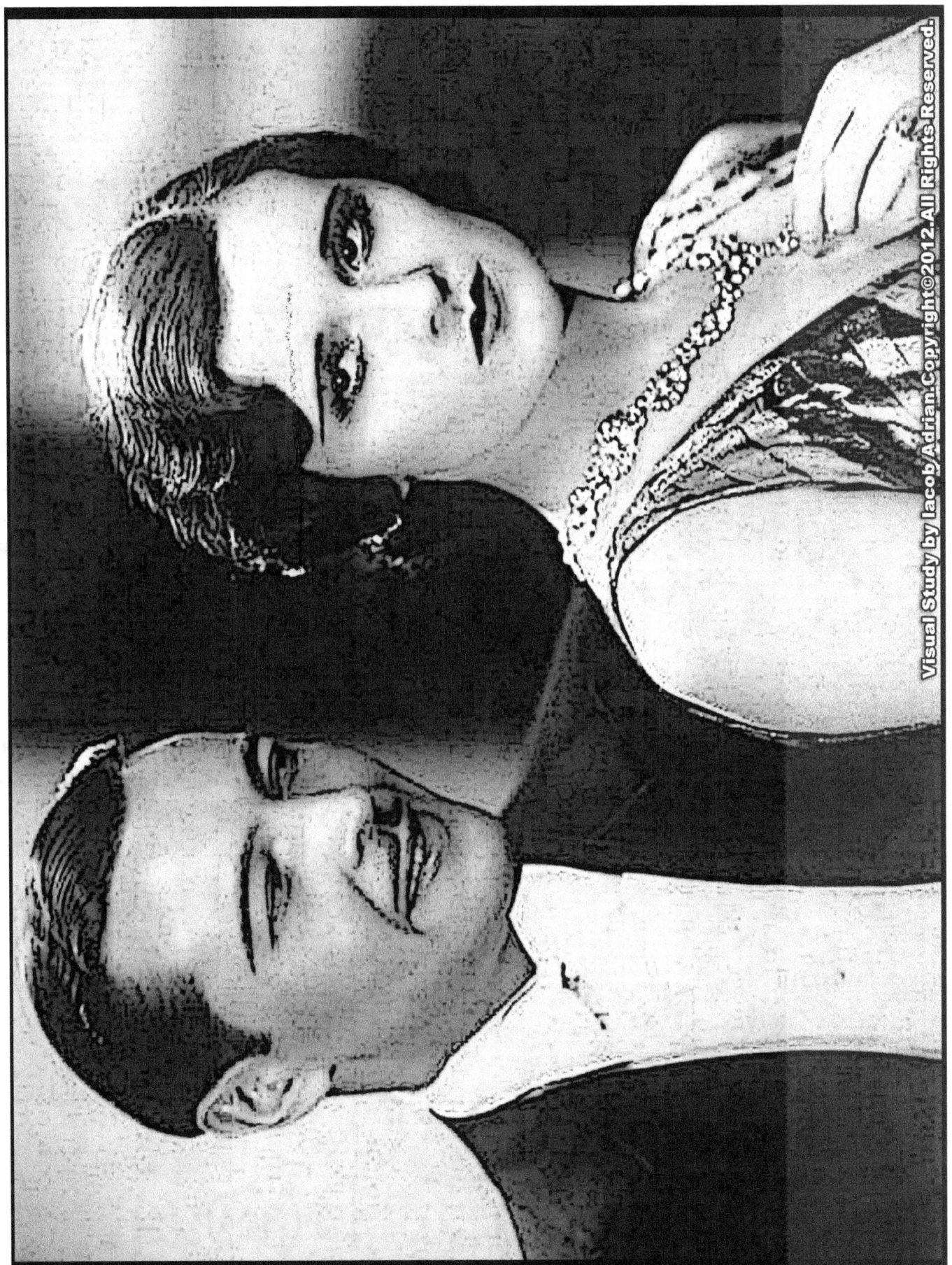

Bird of Paradise (1932)

Bibliographic sources :

A Farewell to Arms (1932)
Bear Shooters (1930)
Beau Brummel (1924)
Behind Office Doors (1931)
Bird of Paradise (1932)
Danger Lights (1930)
Disorder in the Court (1936)
Gulliver's Travels (1939)
Jungle Book (1942)
La Ciociara (Two Women) (1960)
Meet John Doe (1941)
Night of the Living Dead (1968)
Of Human Bondage (1934)
Private Snafu (1943–1946)
Swing High, Swing Low (1937)
The Animal Kingdom (1932)
The General (1926)
The Hunchback of Notre Dame (1923)
The Lady Refuses (1931)
The Phantom of the Opera (1925)
The Perils of Pauline (1914)
White Zombie (1932)

This documentary study use, combined in various proportions,
elements from the following categories, forms and subsets :
- fair use
- documentary
- documentary photography
- feature
- journalism
- arts journalism
- visual journalism
- photojournalism
- celebrity photography
in order to :
- employ material as the object of cultural critique ,
- quote to illustrate an argument or point ,
- use material in historical sequence,
providing independent opinion,
using photos, press articles, advertisements,
opinions of fans etc. ...

www.ingramcontent.com/pod-product-compliance
Lightning Source LLC
Chambersburg PA
CBHW061009200526
45171CB00009B/562